EDITORS' NOTES

Concerto for Clarinet and String Orchestra (with Harp and Piano)

In 1947 Aaron Copland received two unusual requests: Benny Goodman offered a commission for a piece for solo clarinet and orchestra; and bandleader Woody Herman requested a piece for his band. Copland could not accept both commissions. He admired Goodman's phenomenal technique and the success of his Carnegie Hall concert of 1938, featuring an integrated jazz sextet. Copland was flattered by Goodman's offer, since the clarinetist had already commissioned several classical composers, such as Bartók and Hindemith, and he showed a strong interest in performing premieres and commissioning new works. Copland, always wary of repeating himself, welcomed the challenge of composing a clarinet concerto. "It might stimulate some fresh ideas," he said, as he accepted the commission from Benny Goodman, "The King of Swing."

Copland was familiar with the clarinet from his use of the instrument in his *Sextet* and other orchestral ensembles, but he doubted ever writing for solo clarinet had it not been for Goodman's commission. He began in his usual way—studying scores and recordings, and scanning his own notebooks for ideas. When he left on a four-month lecture tour in Latin America for the State Department, his notes and recordings traveled with him. Copland hoped to make headway on the new piece and to decide its form and general characteristics. He knew from the start that a bow to jazz was called for, and he hoped also to demonstrate the lyrical qualities of the clarinet.

When in Rio de Janeiro, Copland made some progress on the piece: it would be in two movements (as is his earlier *Piano Concerto*). The contrasting movements would proceed without pause and be connected by a cadenza. The dreamy and melodic first movement, a traditional ABA form, is in three quarter time, a meter unusual for Copland. From Rio, he wrote to a friend, "The *pas de deux* will make them weep." Upon his return from Latin America, Copland went no further with the piece. He claims to have been "stuck" for musical ideas for the jazzy second movement, except for a Brazilian folk tune and some Latin American rhythms in his head that refused to germinate.

Waiting for him at home was an offer from his agent in Hollywood for music for John Steinbeck's "The Red Pony." The clarinet piece was put aside. Copland worked on the *Concerto* sporadically while at Tanglewood in the summer of 1948 and completed it at home in Sneden's Landing in October 1948. The *Concerto* was dedicated to Benny Goodman and a full score was sent off to him with a recording of a two-piano arrangement. Then followed the anxious time when a composer delivers a new piece and waits for the verdict. Copland heard briefly from Goodman who wrote to say, "With a little editing, I know we will have a good piece." Goodman said in a later interview, "I made no demands on what Copland should write...except that I should have a two year exclusivity on playing the work…I paid two thousand dollars and that's real money…"

The two musicians did not work together during the composition of the *Concerto*. Copland described their first read-through at which Copland played from his piano arrangement: "Benny had the clarinetist David Oppenheim around for moral support. I had written the last page too high, so it had to come down a step. Benny made a few other suggestions—one concerned a high note in the cadenza (I knew Benny could reach that high because I had listened to his recordings). He explained, although he could comfortably reach that high when playing for an audience, he might not be able to if he had to read it from a score for a recording. Therefore, we changed it." The changes were approved by Copland and included in the publication of the *Concerto*.

To Copland's surprise, Goodman delayed the first performance several times. It finally took place 6 November 1950 as a radio broadcast by the NBC Symphony of the Air, Fritz Reiner conducting. The first public performance was by the Philadelphia Orchestra, Eugene Ormandy conducting, Ralph McLane soloist (28 November 1950). The immediate reception was not enthusiastic, but soon clarinetists were welcoming this new virtuoso piece, and it has become a standard in the orchestral repertoire. Goodman and Copland made two recordings for Columbia; most agree the 1960 is better. Goodman said, "Of all the concertos I commissioned, the Copland is performed most…it's a very popular piece."

Although Copland did not provide directions for *ad lib.* sections in the cadenza, players vary on interpretations, some staying close to the published score; others exploiting the "hot" jazz improvisation for which the clarinet is noted. Copland has placed fragments from the fast movement in the cadenza preceding the second movement which he described as a "free Rondo, ending with a fairly elaborate coda as it rushes to end with a typical jazz glissando or smear."

The several changes made to suit Goodman in the fast movement have resulted in two versions of the *Concerto*—Copland's original and the published score with Goodman's requested changes. (Copland had made them somewhat grudgingly in deference to Goodman.) Clarinetists have taken sides on their preferences. The aim of this publication is to provide both versions in published form to be available for choice by performers and conductors: The published edition incorporating the changes requested by Goodman is presented along with the differences from the earlier 1948 manuscript version appearing as *ossias,* as follows:

1. mm. 112-114: In order to allow the soloist some respite before the beginning of the cadenza, the soloist may pause after m. 114 and the harp play the passage in small notes while the strings sustain the chord. A still longer respite may be provided by one solo viola playing the clarinet passage from m. 112, 3rd beat. This *ossia* was, in fact, present in the published version of the score.

AARON COPLAND

CONCERTO FOR CLARINET
and String Orchestra, with Harp and Piano

REDUCTION FOR CLARINET AND PIANO
with ossias from the 1948 manuscript edition

BOOSEY & HAWKES

www.boosey.com
www.halleonard.com

Published by Boosey & Hawkes, Inc.
229 West 28th Street, 11th Floor
New York NY 10001

www.boosey.com

ISMN 979-0-051-58008-8

Notesetting by Philip Rothman
First printed 1952
Second printing August 2013
Corrected July 2019

2. Cadenza, 4th and 3rd measures before m. 120: The passage was originally intended to continue scalewise up to A6 and B6 (a''' and b''', notated for B♭ clarinet as b''' and c♯''''), rather than make a reverse turn as was requested by Goodman. The higher notes are provided as an *ossia*.

3. mm. 441-473: The original solo clarinet passage, restored from the 1948 manuscript version, is provided as an *ossia*. If the *ossia* is taken, the right hand of the orchestral piano part should be omitted from mm. 441-464, to avoid unnecessary doubling with the solo part. If playing the piano reduction, omit the two passages marked *"omit for ossia"* at mm. 441-442 and mm. 445-446.

4. mm. 503-504: Copland had originally intended for these measures to be written G♯6 and B6 (g♯''' and b''', notated for B♭ clarinet as a♯''' and c♯''''). At Goodman's request, these notes were revised downward. The higher notes are provided as an *ossia*.

— Vivian Perlis and Philip Rothman

Notes:

1. All quotations from Copland and Benny Goodman are from interviews with Vivian Perlis, Yale University, Oral History of American Music.

2. See Robert Adelson, "Too Difficult for Benny Goodman," *The Clarinet* (November-December 1995) 42-45.

for Benny Goodman

CONCERTO FOR CLARINET
and String Orchestra, with Harp and Piano

Arranged for clarinet and piano
by the composer

AARON COPLAND
(1948)

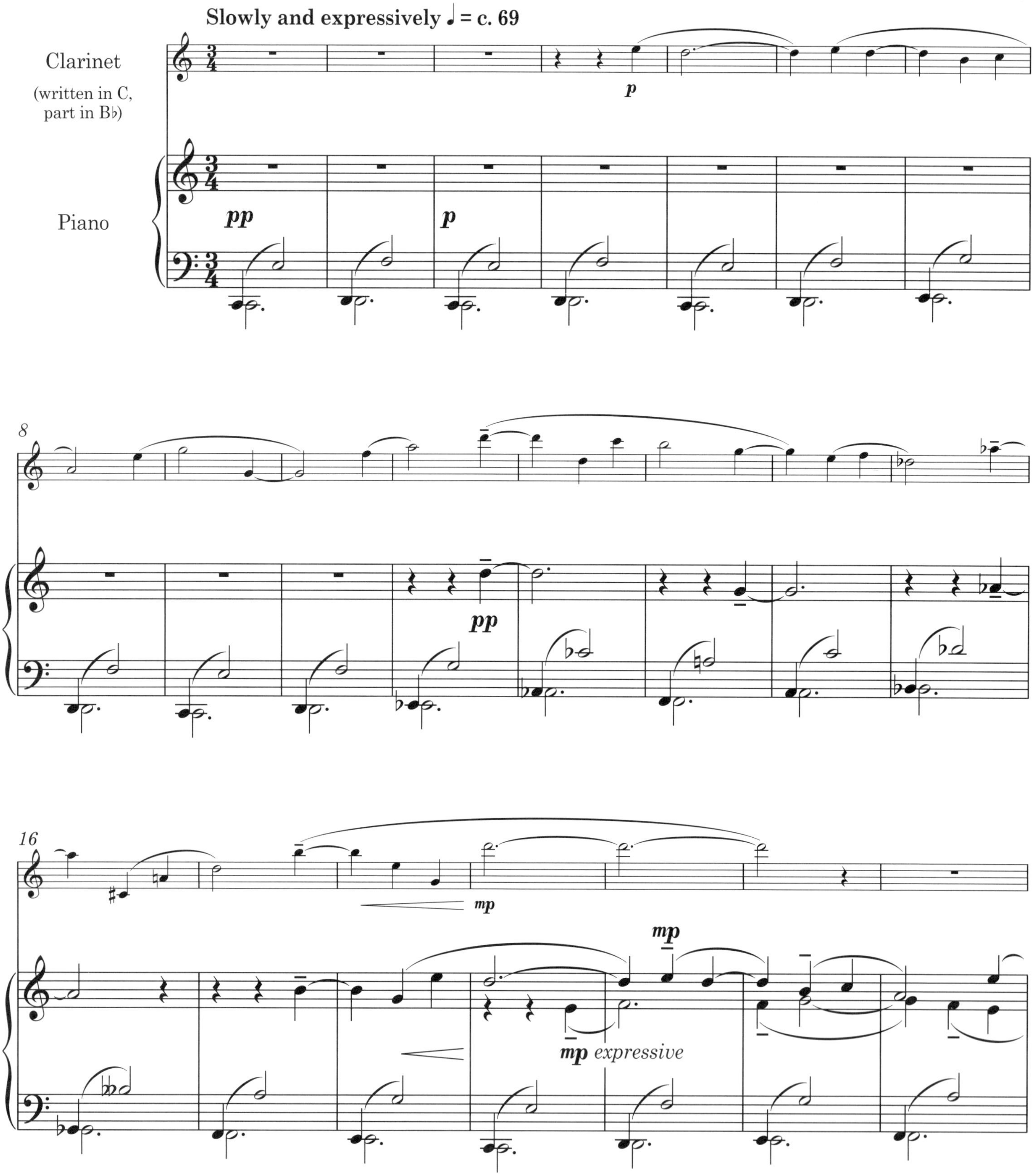

23
mf
mf
mp
29
poco rit.
a tempo
p
p
36
moving forward
p
p
mp
mp
44
rit.
a tempo
mf
p
poco cresc.
mf
p
poco cresc.

Somewhat faster ♩ = 76

70
Broader
mf
mf
f
f
75
rit.
Tempo I ♩ = c. 69
mp
mf
mp
mf
p
p
mp molto
espr.
81
moving forward
mp
mp
88
rit.
a tempo
mf
mp
poco cresc.
mf
mp
poco cresc.

In order to allow the soloist some respite before the beginning of the cadenza, the soloist may pause after bar 114 and the harp play the passage in small notes while the strings sustain the chord. A still longer respite may be provided by one solo viola playing the clarinet passage from bar 112, 3rd beat.

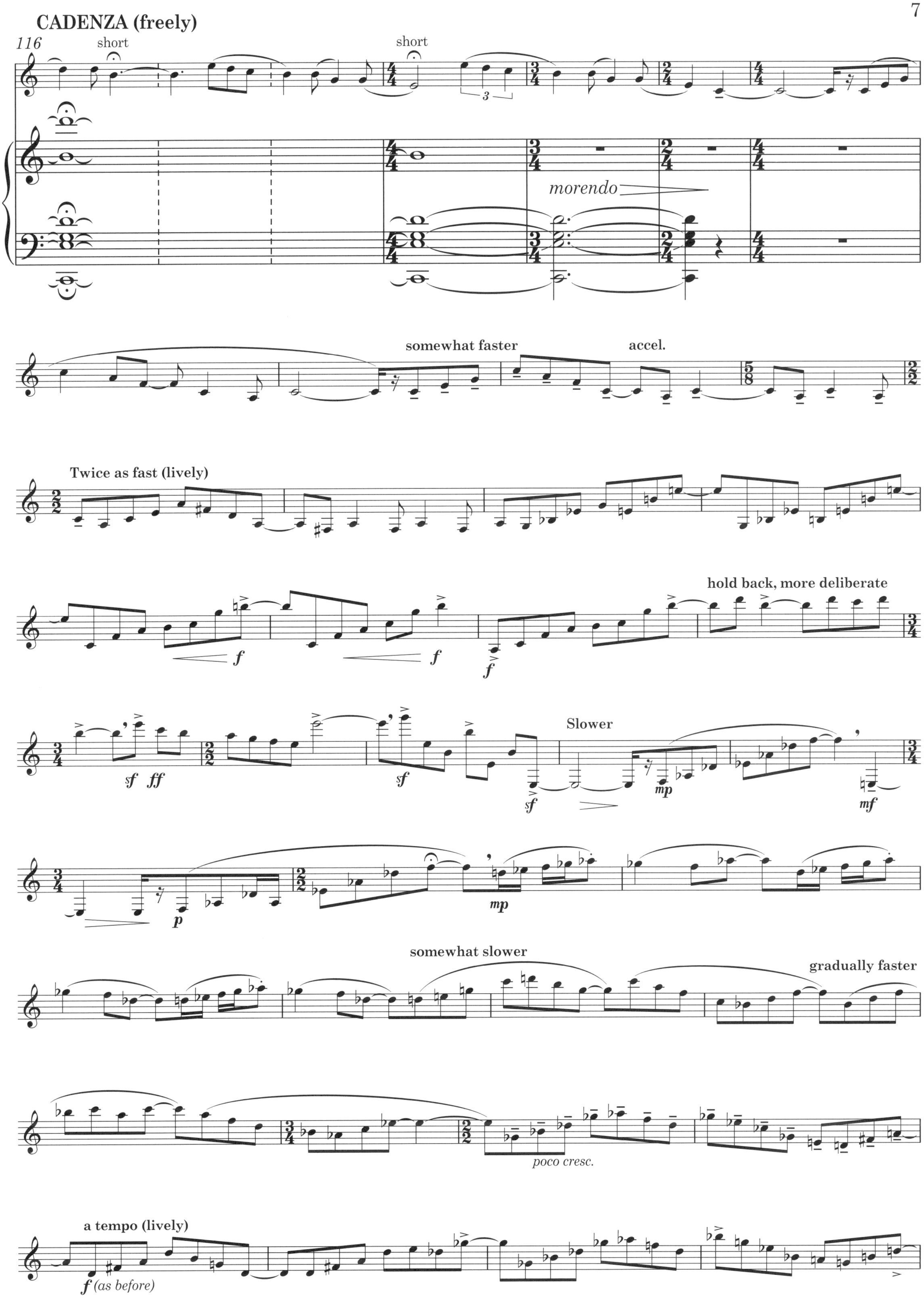
CADENZA (freely)
116
short
short
3
morendo
somewhat faster
accel.
Twice as fast (lively)
f
f
f
hold back, more deliberate
sf
ff
sf
sf
Slower
mp
mf
p
mp
somewhat slower
gradually faster
poco cresc.
a tempo (lively)
f (as before)

* Higher notes *ossia;* from the 1948 manuscript version.

Rather fast ♩ = 120-126
120
p
pp staccato, delicate, wraith-like
mp
8va
pp stacc.
126
Orch.
8va
(8)
8va
132
8va
sf
più f (mf)
sff
136
mf
sf
sff
sff

140
(Orch.)
sff
144
𝅘𝅥 = 𝅗𝅥
f staccatissimo
8va
8va
8va
149
Solo
f staccatissimo
8va
154
stacc.

159
mf
mf
164
poco cresc.
poco cresc.
169
f
f
cresc.
cresc.
174
ff
ff sf heavy stacc.
sf
sf

178
mf
sf
sf mf
sim.
f
182
mf
f
186
♩ = ♩ (♩ = 120)
p
p
p
190
p
p

194
f
f stacc. (forceful)
198
sf
sf
202
p quietly
sf
sf
206
p
mp
mp
13

210
p
mp
214
pp delicate
218
222
f sub.

226
Orch.
ff vigoroso
230
234
dim.
dim.
8va
238
Solo
mp elegantly
p elegantly
(8)

258
263
Trifle faster ♩ = 132
♩ = ♪
268
pp delicate
f sub.
sf * marc.   sf   sf   sf   sf   sf
274
f marc.
sf   sf   sf   sf   sf   sf
* exaggerate all sf's.

297
Same tempo ♩ = 132
with humor, relaxed
mp
f secco
mp
302
307
poco accel.
♩ = 144
mp
mp lightly
p
311
mf
mf

315
a tempo ♩ = 132
mp
p
mp
319
sff
323
(♩ = 132)
Orch.
f
f
327
Solo
mf
mf
mf sim.

poco accel.
332
♩ = 144
337
mp
p
p
342
f
f
p
346
p
p
mp

22
350
353
f
marc.
crude, emphatic
357
361
p suave

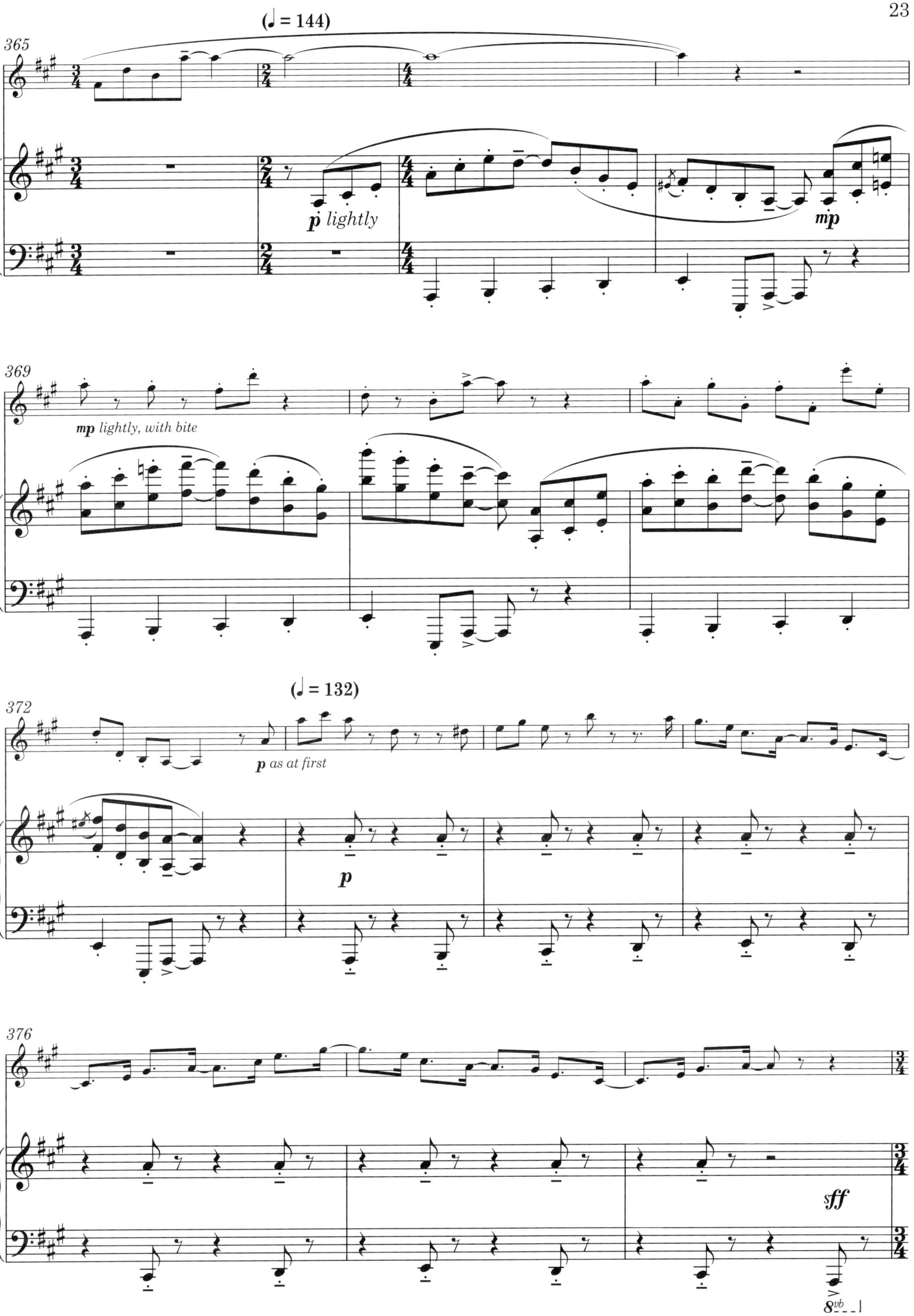
(♩ = 144)
365
p lightly
mp
369
mp lightly, with bite
(♩ = 132)
372
p as at first
p
376
sff
8vb

379
(♩ = ♩)
Orch.
mf ritmico
cresc.
383
ff secco
387
391
sf * mf marc. sf
sf
sf
sf
* exaggerate all sf's.

396
400
404
408

Solo
f ritmico
mf sub.
cresc.
ff marc.
ff sf
sf
sf
sf
sf
sf
sf
sf
sf
sf
sf
sf
sf
sf
sf
sf
sf
sf
ff marc.
e intensivo
ff marc. e intensivo

* The ossia passage from mm. 441-473 is from the 1948 manuscript version.

474
f not too fast
sf
Tempo I ♩ = 120
478
f
483
With emphasis ♩ = 108
488
ff forcefully

* Higher notes *ossia;* from the 1948 manuscript version.

SOLO CLARINET in B♭

NEW EDITION

AARON COPLAND

CONCERTO FOR CLARINET
and String Orchestra, with Harp and Piano

REDUCTION FOR CLARINET AND PIANO
with ossias from the 1948 manuscript edition

BOOSEY & HAWKES

EXCLUSIVELY DISTRIBUTED BY

HAL•LEONARD®

7777 W. BLUEMOUND RD. P.O. BOX 13819 MILWAUKEE, WI 53213

www.boosey.com
www.halleonard.com

SOLO CLARINET in B♭
CONCERTO FOR CLARINET
and String Orchestra, with Harp and Piano
AARON COPLAND
(1948)
Slowly and expressively ♩ = c. 69
Hp., 15ba
p
mp
22–23
mf
poco rit.
a tempo
p
p
moving forward
rit.
mp
mf
a tempo
p
poco cresc.
Somewhat faster ♩ = 76
f
dim.
mp

In order to allow the soloist some respite before the beginning of the cadenza, the soloist may pause after bar 114 and the harp play a passage in bars 114A and 114B while the strings sustain the chord. A still longer respite may be provided by one solo viola playing the clarinet passage from bar 112, 3rd beat.

CADENZA (freely)
116
short
short
119
somewhat faster   accel.
Twice as fast (lively)
hold back, more deliberate
sf ff
sf
sf
Slower
mp
mf
p
mp
somewhat slower
gradually faster
poco cresc.
a tempo (lively)
f (as before)
mf

* Higher notes *ossia;* from the 1948 manuscript version.

125
Vn. I 8va
12
130–141
142
Vn. I 8va
♩ = ♩
147
ƒ staccatissimo
151
3
152–154
158
162
mf
166
poco cresc.
ƒ
170
cresc.
174
♩ = ♩
2
ff
177–178

179
mf
f
183
mf
f
♩ = ♩ (♩ = 120)
187
p
191
195
f
3
196–198
Vn. I
4
201–204
205
p quietly
mp
209
p
213
217
221
5
223–227
8
228–235

Vn. I 8va
mp elegantly
p
mp
p
pp
p
Trifle faster ♩ = 132
♩ = ♪
3
270–272
sf
f marc.

284
ff marc.
sf
sf
289
sf
sf
sf
293
Same tempo ♩ = 132
sf
f
with humor, relaxed
298
mp
302
305
poco accel.
mp
309
♩ = 144
mf
313
mp
317
a tempo ♩ = 132
p
321
(♩ = 132)

SOLO CLARINET in B♭

388
391–394
396–402
404
Vn. I
410
f ritmico
415
ff marc.
420
sf sf sf sf sf
426
429
ff marc. e intensivo
433
sf sf sf sf
437
sf

* The *ossia* passage from mm. 441-473 is from the 1948 manuscript version.

* Higher notes *ossia;* from the 1948 manuscript version.